T-REX WOULD NOT make a GOOD KNIGHT

by Thomas Kingsley Troupe

illustrated by Steph Calvert

PICTURE WINDOW BOOKS
a capstone imprint

RÉSUMÉ

JULIE T-REX

50 Edge Lane
Big Jaw, MP 40052

LENGTH	About 40 feet (12 meters)
HEIGHT	About 15-20 ft (4.6-6m)
WEIGHT	9 tons (8,160 kilograms)
EXPERIENCE AS A KNIGHT	It's a long story.
REFERENCE	NOT this guy

For Phil - Your cardboard armor, paper swords, and boundless creativity are an inspiration. You are amazing. Love, Steph

Dinosaur Daydreams is published by
Picture Window Books, a Capstone Imprint
1710 Roe Crest Drive
North Mankato, MN 56003
www.mycapstone.com

Copyright © 2018 Picture Window Books

Library of Congress Cataloging-in-Publication data
is available on the Library of Congress website.

ISBN: 978-1-5158-2126-7 (library binding)
ISBN: 978-1-5158-2130-4 (paperback)
ISBN: 978-1-5158-2138-0 (eBook PDF)

Summary: So what if her arms are extremely short? Julie the T-Rex wants to be a knight, and she's ready to prove herself to the king. Discussion questions, an interactive look-and-find section, and dinosaur facts complete this fun picture book from the Dinosaur Daydreams series.

Image Credit: Capstone: Jon Hughes, 23

Editor: CHRISTIANNE JONES
Designer: ASHLEE SUKER
Illustrator: STEPH CALVERT

Printed and bound in the USA.
010853S18

Greetings, good sirs and madams!
I'm **Julie** T-Rex. I was just dismissed
from my job as a knight. Was it justified?
You be the judge.

My first day as a knight was really tricky. I got yelled at for drinking some water outside the castle. And the front door was really tight. I didn't mean to wreck the place, but they don't make castles like they used to!

Sir Robert told me knights needed to wear armor. No way would a helmet fit on my giant head! And trying to hide my tail? **FORGET ABOUT IT!**

A knight needs to be an expert with a sword.
But I have two fingers with claws and very short
arms, so I needed help picking up my blade.
Sir Robert said I was a **LOUSY** partner.
Maybe I just needed a longer sword?

Sir Robert said every knight must have a horse, so he took me to the stables to pick out a horse. The horses were so afraid to carry me they all pooped a little bit. Come on! I'm not THAT heavy! **SO RUDE!**

King Samuel wanted to watch the knights joust. We took our places at opposite ends of the arena. Because I didn't have a horse, I just ran at my opponent. Maybe I shouldn't have roared?

TEAM DINOSAUR

The royal family invited all of the knights to a big feast. I just wanted the meat. I took a pretty big bite because I was really hungry. I am a carnivore, so they shouldn't have been so surprised.

That night I woke up to yelling. A dragon had taken the royal twins! The king sent his knights to rescue his children. Sir Robert told me I shouldn't go. I didn't listen. Who cared if I couldn't pick up sword and my tail knocked things over all the time? The kids were in trouble!

I followed the knights
to a dragon's cave.

17

When the dragon poked his head out, I
recognized that face. It was my cousin, Frank!

I asked Frank to let the kids go. Obviously
he did. Clearly the other knights were not
happy that I was the hero.

Even after I saved the royal twins I was asked to leave. But don't worry. I'll be okay. I'm ready to start my new job as a race car driver. I sure hope my arms will reach the steering wheel!

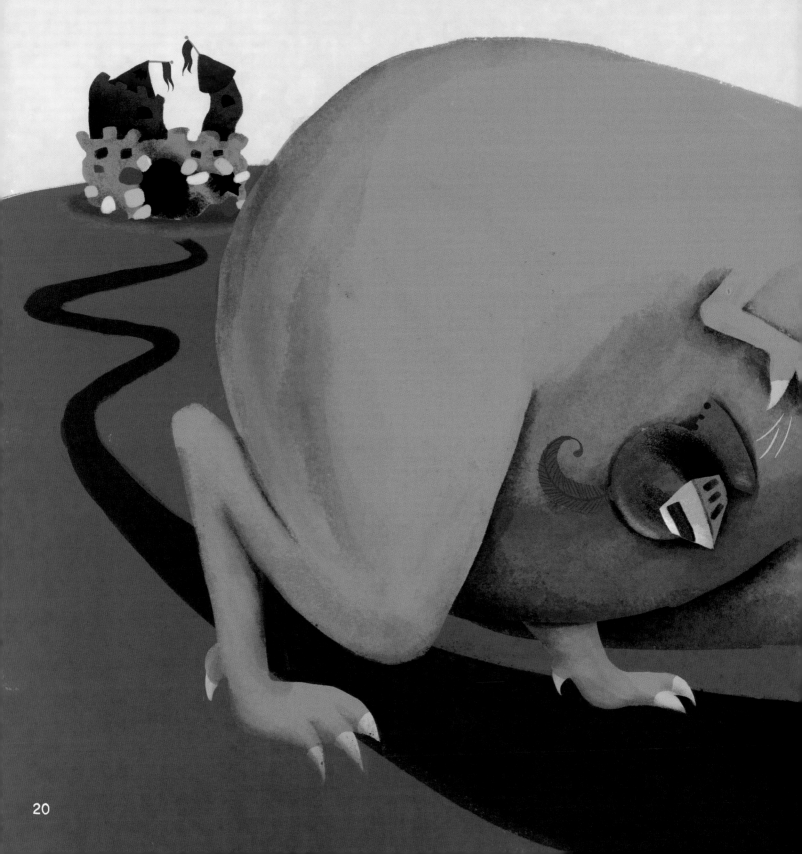

DINO DIG

The answer to each question below is hidden in the art. Each answer is one word or number. Dig through the story until you find the answer. Good luck!

1. Seven T-Rex skeletons have been discovered in what South Dakota city? (page 17)

2. T-Rex is best known for a certain body part. What is it? (page 8)

3. About how much did a T-Rex weigh (in tons)? (page 11)

4. The T-Rex was around 40 feet (12 m) long, or the same length as a popular school vehicle. What is that vehicle? (page 6)

5. The T-Rex only ate meat. What is a meat-eater called? (page 15)

MORE TYRANNOSAURUS REX FACTS

- » The name *Tyrannosaurus* means "tyrant lizard."

- » T-Rex lived more than 65.5 million years ago.

- » It's possible that the T-Rex was covered in fuzzy feathers.

- » T-Rex had great eyesight and the strongest bite of any land animal that has ever lived.

- » Though small, a T-Rex's arms could easily lift around 430 pounds (195 kg).

- » T-Rex had a huge head and used its tail for balance.

DINO DISCUSSION

1. Would you rather be a knight or a dinosaur? Why?

2. Do you think it was smart of Julie to go on the rescue mission, even when she was told not to? Why or why not?

3. What job do you think a T-Rex should have? Why?

DINO GLOSSARY

carnivore – an animal that only eats meat

claws – sharp curved parts on the toe or fingers of an animal

T-Rex – the shortened version of Tyrannosaurus Rex

KNIGHT GLOSSARY

arena – a building for sports and other forms of entertainment that has a large area surrounded by seats

armor – special clothing that people wear to protect their bodies from weapons

joust – to fight with swords while riding a horse

opponent – a person, team, or group that is competing against another in a contest